Angel Whispers

Paintings by

SANDRA KUCK

Angel Whispers

Text copyright © 2010 by Harvest House Publishers

Artwork copyright © by Sandra Kuck

Published by Harvest House Publishers
Eugene, Oregon 97402
www.harvesthousepublishers.com

ISBN 978-0-7369-2909-7

Design and production by Garborg Design Works, Savage, Minnesota

_____

To

_____

From

_____

Date

THE REASON BIRDS FLY AND WE CAN'T IS
SIMPLY THAT THEY HAVE PERFECT FAITH, FOR
TO HAVE PERFECT FAITH IS TO HAVE WINGS.

SIR JAMES M. BARRIE

What sunshine is to flowers,

smiles are to humanity. These are

but trifles, to be sure; but scattered

along life's pathway, the good

they do is inconceivable.

JOSEPH ADDISON

TO ACCOMPLISH GREAT THINGS,
WE MUST NOT ONLY ACT, BUT ALSO DREAM;
NOT ONLY PLAN, BUT ALSO BELIEVE.

ANATOLE FRANCE

Every
wish
is like
a prayer
to God.

ELIZABETH
BARRETT
BROWNING

A kind word is like a spring day.

RUSSIAN PROVERB

AN ANGEL CAN ILLUMINATE
THE THOUGHT AND MIND OF
MAN BY STRENGTHENING THE
POWER OF VISION.

SAINT THOMAS AQUINAS

But let all who take

refuge in you be glad;

let them ever sing for joy.

Spread your protection

over them, that those

who love your name may

rejoice in you.

PSALM 5:11

JUST LIVING IS NOT ENOUGH.
ONE MUST HAVE SUNSHINE,
FREEDOM, AND A LITTLE FLOWER.

HANS CHRISTIAN ANDERSEN

Go confidently in the direction of your dreams! Live the life you've imagined.

HENRY DAVID THOREAU

YOU ASPIRE TO GREAT THINGS?

CUT A PATH INTO
THE HEAVEN OF GLORY
LEAVING A TRACK OF
LIGHT FOR MEN
TO WONDER AT.

WILLIAM BLAKE

The natural flights of the
human mind are not from
pleasure to pleasure but
from hope to hope.

SAMUEL JOHNSON

BEGIN WITH LITTLE ONES.

Gratitude is a soil on which joy thrives.

BERTHOLD AUERBACH

Sweet souls around us watch us still,

Press nearer to our side;

Into our thoughts, into our prayers,

With gentle helpings glide.

HARRIET BEECHER STOWE

9

FIND YOUR PURPOSE AND FLING YOUR LIFE OUT
INTO IT; AND THE LOFTIER YOUR PURPOSE IS, THE
MORE SURE YOU WILL BE TO MAKE THE WORLD
RICHER WITH EVERY ENRICHMENT OF YOURSELF.

PHILLIPS BROOKS

Far away there in the sunshine
are my highest aspirations. I
may not reach them but I can look
up and see their beauty, believe in
them, and try to follow them.

LOUISA MAY ALCOTT

*Seeing,
hearing, feeling,
are miracles, and
each part and
tag of me is a
miracle.*

Walt Whitman

Happiness is a glory shining
far down upon us from
heaven. She is a divine
dew, which the soul feels
dropping upon it from the
amaranth bloom and golden
fruitage of paradise.

CHARLOTTE BRONTË

WE CARRY
WITH US THE
WONDERS
WE SEEK
WITHOUT US.

SIR THOMAS BROWNE

To travel hopefully is a

THERE IS ONLY ONE
HAPPINESS IN LIFE, TO
LOVE AND BE LOVED.

GEORGE SAND

All God's pleasures are
simple ones; the rapture of a
May morning sunshine, the
stream blue and green, kind
words, benevolent acts, the
glow of good humor.

F.W. ROBERTSON

Have you had a kindness shown?

Pass it on;

'Twas not given for thee alone,

Pass it on;

Let it travel down the years,

Let it wipe another's tears,

'Til in Heaven the deed appears—

Pass it on.

HENRY BURTON

THE BEST PORTION OF
A GOOD MAN'S LIFE—
HIS LITTLE, NAMELESS,
UNREMEMBERED ACTS OF
KINDNESS AND LOVE.

WILLIAM WORDSWORTH

BETTER THING THAN TO ARRIVE.

ROBERT LOUIS STEVENSON

Folly ends where genuine hope begins.

WILLIAM COWPER

CLOSE TO MY HEART I FOLD
EACH LOVELY THING...
THE SWEET DAY YIELDS;
AND NOT DISCONSOLATE...
WITH CALM IMPATIENCE
OF THE WOODS, I WAIT...
FOR LEAF AND BLOSSOM,
WHEN GOD GIVES US SPRING.

JOHN GREENLEAF WHITTIER

The beauty of the world and the orderly arrangement of everything celestial makes us confess that there is an excellent and eternal nature, which ought to be worshiped and admired by all mankind.

CICERO

One joy scatters a hundred griefs.

CHINESE PROVERB

The level of
our success
is limited
only by our
imagination
and no act
of kindness,
however
small,
is ever
wasted.

AESOP

17

ANGELS DESCENDING, BRING FROM ABOVE,
ECHOES OF MERCY, WHISPERS OF LOVE.

FANNY J. CROSBY

Ask and you will

BOLDLY AND WISELY IN
THAT LIGHT THOU HAST—
THERE IS A HAND ABOVE
WILL HELP THEE ON.

PHILIP JAMES BAILEY

Sing out my soul,
thy songs of joy;
Such as a happy bird
will sing,
Beneath a Rainbow's
lovely arch,
In early spring.

WILLIAM HENRY DAVIES

receive, and your joy will be complete.

JOHN 16:24

Nothing
but heaven
itself is better
than a friend
who is really
a friend.

PLAUTUS

What sweet delight

a quiet life affords.

WILLIAM DRUMMOND

**WHAT IS TO REACH
THE HEART MUST
COME FROM ABOVE.**

LUDWIG VAN BEETHOVEN

In every exalted joy, there

mingles a sense of gratitude.

MARIE VON EBNER-ESCHENBACH

*Hope is the
word which
God has
written on
the brow of
every man.*

VICTOR HUGO

21

LOVE IS PATIENT, LOVE IS KIND.
IT DOES NOT ENVY, IT DOES NOT BOAST,
IT IS NOT PROUD. IT IS NOT RUDE,
IT IS NOT SELF-SEEKING.
IT IS NOT EASILY ANGERED,
IT KEEPS NO RECORD OF WRONGS.
LOVE DOES NOT DELIGHT IN EVIL,
BUT REJOICES WITH THE TRUTH.
IT ALWAYS PROTECTS, ALWAYS TRUSTS,
ALWAYS HOPES, ALWAYS PERSEVERES.
LOVE NEVER FAILS.

1 CORINTHIANS 13:4-8

What one has wished for in youth, in old age one has in abundance.

JOHANN WOLFGANG von GOETHE

24

BE INSPIRED WITH THE BELIEF THAT LIFE IS
A GREAT AND NOBLE CALLING; NOT A MEAN
AND GROVELING THING THAT WE ARE TO
SHUFFLE THROUGH AS WE CAN, BUT AN
ELEVATED AND LOFTY DESTINY.

WILLIAM E. GLADSTONE

*Of all the things which wisdom
provides to make life entirely happy,
much the greatest is the possession
of friendship.*

EPICURUS

Happy is the
house that
shelters a
friend.

RALPH WALDO EMERSON

A SINGLE GRATEFUL THOUGHT TOWARDS
HEAVEN IS THE MOST PERFECT PRAYER.

EPHRAIM GOTTHOLD LESSING

*Happiness is like a butterfly
which, when pursued,
is always beyond our grasp,
but, if you will sit down quietly,
may alight upon you.*

NATHANIEL HAWTHORNE

FRIENDS ARE THE SUNSHINE OF LIFE.

JOHN HAY

*To reach the port of
heaven, we must sail
sometimes with the wind,
and sometimes against
it, but we sail, and not
drift, nor live at anchor.*

OLIVER WENDELL HOLMES

*A cheerful look
brings joy to the heart,
and good news gives
health to the bones.*

PROVERBS 15:30

Our aspirations are our possibilities.

SAMUEL JOHNSON

27

There is
nothing like a
dream to create
the future.

VICTOR HUGO

For all we know
Of what the Blessed do above
Is, that they sing,
and that they love.

EDMUND WALLER

A friend is a gift you give yourself.

ROBERT LOUIS STEVENSON

MUSIC IS WELL SAID TO BE
THE SPEECH OF ANGELS.

THOMAS CARLYLE

I BELIEVE THAT IF ONE ALWAYS
LOOKED AT THE SKY, ONE
WOULD END UP WITH WINGS.

GUSTAVE FLAUBERT

THE BEST AND
MOST BEAUTIFUL
THINGS IN THIS
WORLD CANNOT
BE SEEN OR
EVEN HEARD,
BUT MUST BE FELT
WITH THE HEART.

HELEN KELLER

*Let us not be
justices of the peace,
but angels of peace.*

SAINT THERESA OF LISIEUX

TEACH US DELIGHT IN SIMPLE THINGS.

RUDYARD KIPLING

*The heart that is
to be filled to the
brim with holy joy
must be held still.*

GEORGE SEATON BOWES

I like the dreams of the future better than the history of the past.

Thomas Jefferson

31

Perfume and incense bring joy to the heart, and the pleasantness of one's friend springs from his earnest counsel.

PROVERBS 27:9

If instead of a gem, or even a flower, we should cast the gift of a loving thought into the heart of a friend, that would be giving as the angels give.

GEORGE MACDONALD

If I have freedom in my love,
And in my soul am free,
Angels alone that soar above,
Enjoy such liberty.

RICHARD LOVELACE

The soul without
imagination is what
an observatory would
be without a telescope.

HENRY WARD BEECHER

HOPE IS
THE DREAM
OF A SOUL
AWAKE.

FRENCH PROVERB

35

GRATITUDE IS A NICE
TOUCH OF BEAUTY
ADDED LAST OF ALL TO
THE COUNTENANCE,
GIVING A CLASSIC
BEAUTY, AN ANGELIC
LOVELINESS, TO THE
CHARACTER.

THEODORE PARKER

WITHOUT FAITH
A MAN CAN DO
NOTHING; WITH
IT ALL THINGS ARE
POSSIBLE.

SIR WILLIAM OSLER

Sweet sleep,
with soft down
Weave thy brows
an infant crown!
Sweet sleep,
angel mild,
Hover o'er
my happy child.

WILLIAM BLAKE

Hope springs eternal in the human breast.

ALEXANDER POPE

I cannot be content with less than heaven.

PHILIP JAMES BAILEY

38

Let every dawn of morning be to you as the beginning of life, and every setting sun be to you as its close, then let every one of these short lives leave its sure record of some kindly thing done for others, some goodly strength or knowledge gained for yourself.

John Ruskin

Welcome it in every fair face, every fair sky, every fair flower.

Ralph Waldo Emerson

Joys are our wings, sorrows are our spurs.

Jean Paul Richter

How rare and wonderful is that flash of a moment when we realize we have discovered a friend.

William E. Rothschild

HOPE IS THAT THING WITH FEATHERS
THAT PERCHES IN THE SOUL
AND SINGS THE TUNE WITHOUT THE
WORDS AND NEVER STOPS... AT ALL.

EMILY DICKINSON

An aspiration is a joy forever.

ROBERT LOUIS STEVENSON

YOU HAVE MADE KNOWN
TO ME THE PATH OF LIFE;
YOU WILL FILL ME WITH
JOY IN YOUR PRESENCE.

PSALM 16:11

Light tomorrow
with today.

Elizabeth Barrett Browning

The sight of the stars
makes me dream.

The grand essentials of happiness are: something to do, something to love, and something to hope for.

ALLAN K. CHALMERS

IS IT SO SMALL A THING
TO HAVE ENJOYED
THE SUN,
TO HAVE LIVED LIGHT
IN THE SPRING,
TO HAVE LOVED,
TO HAVE THOUGHT,
TO HAVE DONE?

MATTHEW ARNOLD

Hope is the only good which is common to all men;
those who have nothing more possess hope still.

THALES OF MILETUS

A good character is the best tombstone. Those who loved you and were helped by you will remember you when forget-me-nots have withered. Carve your name on hearts, not on marble.

CHARLES H. SPURGEON

DREAMS ARE THE TOUCHSTONES OF OUR CHARACTER.

HENRY DAVID THOREAU

Never lose an opportunity to see anything that is beautiful. It is God's handwriting— a wayside sacrament. Welcome it in every fair face, every fair sky, every fair flower.

RALPH WALDO EMERSON

FAITH IS DARING THE SOUL TO GO BEYOND WHAT THE EYES CAN SEE.

WILLIAM NEWTON CLARK

I have loved my
friends as
I do virtue,
my soul, my God.

Sir Thomas Browne

My voice shalt
thou hear in
the morning,
O Lord;
in the morning
will I direct
my prayer
unto thee, and
will look up.

Psalm 5:3 kjv

Oh, be my friend, and

46

The rays of
happiness, like those
of light, are colorless
when unbroken.

HENRY WADSWORTH LONGFELLOW

THE TRUEST GREATNESS
LIES IN BEING KIND, THE
TRUEST WISDOM IN A
HAPPY MIND.

ELLA WHEELER WILCOX

HOPE IS LIKE THE WING
OF AN ANGEL, SOARING
UP TO HEAVEN,
AND BEARING OUR
PRAYERS TO THE
THRONE OF GOD.

JEREMY TAYLOR

teach me to be thine!

RALPH WALDO EMERSON

47

$\mathcal{M}$ay the road rise up to meet you,
May the wind be always at your back,
May the sun shine warm upon your face,
And rains fall soft upon your fields.
And until we meet again,
May God hold you in the palm of His hand.

IRISH BLESSING